The 10 Best Practices for Managing Remote Workers

Supervising in the New Normal -
Remote Working is Here to Stay.

Dr. M. Paula Daoust
www.BehaviorTransitions.com

The 10 Best Practices for Managing Remote Workers:
Supervising in the New Normal - Remote Working is Here to Stay.

Dr. M. Paula Daoust

Copyright © 2021 Maplewheat Publishing

Cover design by Germancreative

ISBN: ISBN: 978-0-9778955-6-4

First Printing: July 2021

Written by a Leading Expert
with 30 Years' Experience

Dr. M. Paula Daoust has a doctorate in Behavior Psychology and is an expert in helping people find and maintain their peak performance. She is also a certified hypnotherapist and seamlessly blends these tools into her coaching to help people easily achieve lasting change. Over 25 years, she has taught hundreds of master-level students how to be more persuasive and influential, and how to successfully manage conflict.

Dr. M. Paula Daoust is the expert other leaders look to for help in finding their peak performance. She has taught workshops and spoken at events all over North America on subjects such as conflict, change management, storytelling, influence and power, anxiety and stress at work, and peak performance.

www.BehaviorTransitions.com
Call (785) 633-6078

Other Books by Dr. Daoust

Conflict at Work:
A Toolkit for Managing Your Emotions for Successful Results.

◇◇◇

Conflict at Work:
The Companion Workbook

◇◇◇

I CAN Speak:
*Conquering fear and building confidence
in high-stakes speaking situations.*

◇◇◇

Using Emotional Intelligence In Sales:
*Unlocking the Secrets of Your Subconscious
(Co-authored with Michael G. Eichten)*

◇◇◇

Using Emotional Intelligence in Sales:
The Supplementary Workbook

Table of Contents

Chapter One

The New Normal..1

Chapter Two

The Upside of the Remote Work World...............5

Chapter Three

What's Missing in the World of Remote Work .. 11

Chapter Four

The 10 Best Practices for Managing the Remote
Worker 19

Chapter Five

Facilitating A Hybrid Meeting............................... 35

Chapter Six

The Secret Sauce 47

Supplementary Material

10 Best Practices Summary..................................... 49
7 Strategies for Hybrid Meetings 50
References 51

Dr. M. Paula Daoust

Chapter One
The New Normal

◇◇◇◇◇◇◇◇◇◇◇◇◇◇◇◇◇◇◇◇◇◇◇◇◇◇◇◇◇◇◇◇◇

Jumping in

The business world had been flirting with remote work for several years and some of the most progressive organizations were making it happen. Skeptics, however, were suspicilous of remote workers' work ethic and felt that productivity would slide. In addition, they believed that essential collaboration between and within teams would be hampered.

Despite these fears, some organizations moved forward. They made it happen because the flexibility, which remote work offered its employees was a major contributor to morale and an advantage in recruiting for niche positions. It appeared that the business world was slowly dipping its toe into the waters of remote working. But wading in boldly was still relegated to the more adventurous, younger, smaller and more entrepreneurial companies.

Then the pandemic hit. Survival depended on not just wading in but jumping in with both feet and swimming in the sea of remote work. When it was no longer safe to work side-by-side in the office or meet face-to-face in the conference room, businesses had two choices - allow their people to work from home or shut down completely.

The choice was obvious and overnight it seemed that everyone was working from home. Fortunately, technology had been developing all along. With the plethora of tools for video-conferencing, real-time messaging, and collaborating, the worst of the skeptics' fears were not realized. The biggest issue has not been an inability to communicate but rather learning how to manage the multiple communication channels efficiently.

Embracing Remote Work

Many people had insisted that their work could not be done remotely or that they would not like to work anywhere but in their office. Just as many folks yearned for the opportunity to work from home but recognized that their organization was not open to it.  Being forced into experimenting with this new world, the proverbial Pandora's Box has been opened. Folks have discovered that, with the new technology tools, they CAN do their work from outside of the office. Those who had wanted to do it, but their corporate culture would not permit it, now have evidence that it not only works, but that in many cases it works very well.

Having tested remote work, discovered that it can work, and that many folks liked it, working remotely has become the new normal. Organizations that had historically been skeptical or outright antagonistic to the concept are now embracing it. New terms have surfaced to describe the many versions that have emerged: remote working; virtual workers; situational work locations; flex work; distributed teams; telework; telecommuting; work-at-home workers; rotational schedules; hybrid schedules; and more.

Some of these terms describe the same pattern of virtual work, while others refer to very different patterns and experiences. It doesn't matter what term is used, it's clear that the concept of working virtually is now a reality in most organizations. The names given to the various ways in which remote work manifests itself, is a matter of the organizational culture. But across corporate America, remote work appears here to stay.

The train has left the station

The change is here to stay, whether you fully support this new remote working business environment, or you vehemently disagree with it and dearly want things to return to the pre-pandemic routines and environment. The proverbial Pandora's Box has been opened. With the new technology tools available and personal experience with the new way of doing business, the question is no longer whether to allow remote work or not, but rather, how to make it work better in support of organization's goals.

That is the focus of this book. We will examine both the upside and the downside of this working environment and then discuss best practices that will allow us to maximize the upside and minimize or eliminate the downside. When you begin putting these best practices into play with your team, you will see some immediate benefits. The truly great news is that these practices are not difficult, nor are they completely unfamiliar to you. Most importantly, small changes can have big effects!

Types of Remote Workers

With so many terms for the same thing and some terms that sound the same but really mean something different, it might be helpful to clarify the remote work landscape.

- *Telecommuter / Work-at-Home / Telework / Virtual / Remote worker* – this refers to those workers whose primary work location is at home. It is expected that they will work 40 hours per week from their home office and only come into the main office for specific scheduled meetings or training.

- *Hybrid workers* – these are workers who work a split schedule with pre-designated days working from home and from the office. Each week's schedule is predictable and consistent.

- *Situational workers* – this refers to those workers whose work location will vary, depending on the task. The choice between working from home or in the office is subject to supervisory approval.

- *Distributed Team* - this refers to a team that is generally works from home but is spread out geographically.

Chapter Two
The Upside of the Remote Work World

◇◇◇◇◇◇◇◇◇◇◇◇◇◇◇◇◇◇◇◇◇◇◇◇◇◇◇◇◇◇◇◇◇◇

The good

There are two sides to a coin and before we can begin looking at how to take advantage of this new normal, it might be helpful to understand why we should. Changing just for the sake of change wastes resources and is distressing to those involved. There must be a legitimate benefit in change or the organization would be better off maintaining or returning to the previous status quo.

In the last chapter I suggested that once people experienced remote working first-hand, they would be less willing to return to the office full-time. Why is that? There are several answers to this question and we will explore the seven advantages of working remotely which are cited most often.

1. Increased productivity.

Workers report that they experience fewer distractions at home. Coworkers are not stopping by with gossip, ad hoc work requests or invitations to take a break. The sounds from conversations in neighboring cubicles are absent and they are no longer subjected to the annoying music choice or gum-chewing sounds of their office neighbors. Add this to the com-

fort of their own environment and remote workers report an increased ability to concentrate which translates to faster, more accurate outcomes.

A Stanford University 2-year control group study found that those workers who worked from home produced the equivalent of one extra full day of work each week, compared to the group that continued to work in the office (Mautz, 2018). This is just one study but if you search the internet, you will find many more studies with similar outcomes. These studies support the subjective observation, of both the workers and their supervisors, that many remote workers are more productive at home than in the office. One caveat, as with any study, the findings would apply to many workers, but not all. The results for your team would always depend on the quality of supervision and support provided!

2. Increased flexibility.

Working from home allows parents to get their children off to school without needing to rush out the door themselves and to be physically present when the children come home. If family members are home, lunches can be quality time together. Workers also report that it is

easier to fit exercise in and around their busy schedule because the necessity for an immediate shower might not be as pressing. If a visit from a repairman needs to be arranged, it can be accomplished with little disruption to work flow.

3. No commute.

The average commute to work in the United States is 26 minutes, one-way. If you do the math, working remotely adds up to five hours of quality, prime time, recovered each week. This is time that could be used to learn a new language, master some software, read a book, or even write a book. The possibilities for using this new-found time are as unique as each worker.

The important issue is that this is time retrieved from our schedules during which we are normally at our most alert, most creative, and least tired. Cutting out time spent commuting is stealing back peak time that each worker can use in ways that is most meaningful to them.

4. Less stress.

Greater control over the work environment and better work-life balance can contribute to experiencing less stress. A study done by PGI argued that working from home can reduce stress-levels by as much as 82%. Remote workers' stress levels will vary dramatically, from one to another, but many report that they do feel more in control of their life when working from home.

5. More comfortable.

Working from home also allows more control over the room temperature, music, the choice of colors and decorations in the room, and furniture. When you are working from home, you are surrounded by the things you have chosen and love, including your pets. Looking up from a difficult task and seeing your dog or cat snoozing in their bed beside your desk can be tremendously calming.

Working from home allows more flexibility in clothing. Many folks working from home will have a jacket handy to pull on over a t-shirt for impromptu video-conference meetings. The joke in the media is that many workers are sitting in shorts or pajama bottoms during meetings because just their upper body is visible. In advance of a scheduled meeting, a quick trip to the closet for a swift change from comfortable exercise clothes to the more formal collared shirt is easy to do.

6. Cost-savings.

Cost savings are available to both the worker and the organization. The worker saves money on gas or transportation to and from work. This alone can easily add up to over a $1,000 per year. In addition, lunches at home are less expensive and oftn include using up left-overs from earlier meals.

For the employer, fewer employees in the office means less overhead in terms of office and parking space. There is also less wear and tear

on the building and furniture. Other savings are in the less obvious benefits of coffee bars or providing a subsidized cafeteria. Fewer people in the office means fewer people using these benefits. In addition, some organizations have even found that having remote workers has decreased office supply expenses.

7. Less absenteeism.

It makes sense that with less stress, there would also be less illness. Further, you are exposed to fewer people carrying a range of viruses 6.that can make you sick. But, these are not the only reasons for reduced absenteeism.

For example, folks who suffer from migraine headaches have reported that on days they might have had to call in sick they are able to continue working, taking short breaks to manage their headache. People tend to choose medical services closer to their home than the office and if they are working from home, they can slip out, attend an appointment and return to work. Instead of scheduling a day or half a day to take care of their medical needs, they are using an hour or two.

> Technology now allows people to connect anytime, anywhere, to anyone in the world, from almost any device. This is dramatically changing the way people work, facilitating 24/7 collaboration with colleagues who are dispersed across time zones, countries, and continents.
>
> *Michael Dell*

Chapter Three
What's Missing in the World of Remote Work

◇◇◇◇◇◇◇◇◇◇◇◇◇◇◇◇◇◇◇◇◇◇◇◇◇◇◇◇◇◇◇◇◇◇

The bad

Remote working has become a reality and not only is it here to stay, it's growing. Remote work offers benefits to both the organization and the worker. But, there are downsides which must be acknowledged and then addressed. Here are some of the critical things that are missing when we work remotely.

Small talk is BIG talk

We don't have as many casual conversations because we don't pass each other on the way to the copy machine or the restroom, in the elevator or the halls, and we don't eat lunch together.

Without these brief moments, the opportunity to casually ask about a project, the welfare of a colleague's son who broke his arm, or a

quick check-in on their vacation or return to work after an illness. You don't share concerns about the local football or baseball team's trade or chat about the weather, a new restaurant, or an upcoming community event.

These brief exchanges of niceties might not seem important, but they represent an invitation for an expanded conversation. They can be the bridge to building a deeper, more trusting relationship. They are essential to feeling cared about and connected with the team and the organization.

Leaking emotions

The first language we all learn is body language. Much of this language occurs at the subconscious level and is out of your direct control. When words and body language don't match, you will trust the message you received via the body language channel. A colleague might say they want to cooperate with you but somehow, you know in your gut that you need to keep an eye on this person.

We constantly leak information about our feelings and intentions and, for most of this communication, we cannot mask it. When we are physically in the presence of our colleagues, we can sense when they are confident and when they are hesitant. We can feel when they are energized and when they are discouraged. We often know this about them without consciously being aware that we know it, but it influences the words we choose and the actions we take.

When we are working from home, we depend on video-conferencing, the telephone, or written communication that comes via instant messaging and email. Albert Mehrabian argued that only 7% of a message comes via the words we use. The rest of the message is delivered via vocal tone and body language. Try stressing a different word in the following sentence

and you will recognize how different the message is, depending on which word is stressed: "I want to work with you."

Misunderstandings of written communication are legendary but the telephone and visual-conferencing are only marginally better. The telephone allows for the tonal intonations but without the matching body language, the potential for misunderstanding is still very possible. When video-conferencing is used, you have access to body language evident from large movements but the fine, subtle signals will get lost, depending on the quality of cameras and computer screens.

Incidental information

Another consequence of the absence of unscheduled interactions with colleagues is the loss of incidental information. Some of this information might come in the form of gossip. While we generally look down on gossip, it is important in feeling a part of the team. It also pro-

vides essential warnings about what topics to stay away from, who to talk to and when, and how you should respond to some team members.

Gossip can serve as a roadmap that helps you to avoid emotional landmines, and it can point you to more effective routes for getting things done. Gossip is a part of every group and it is not always an unhealthy behavior. It is also an essential component in developing and maintaining group culture. It provides clues about the unwritten rules and underlying values of the group. While it isn't something you want to actively encourage, it does have a role to play in the group and it's absence makes it harder for members to feel connected to the larger group.

Another kind of information that gets lost when casual interactions are absent is information that can help us move forward on a task or project. Sometimes we don't know what we don't know and, just as important, others might not know what we don't know. Chatting provides a vehicle for information to surface that we didn't know we needed.

Out-of-sight, out-of-mind

We tend to stop thinking about a person if we don't see them for a while. Not only do we stop thinking about them, we can easily underestimate the effort they are investing or the quantity and quality of their outcomes. This can have serious consequences when assigning high profile projects or in considering promotions.

As a result, employees could be left feeling discouraged, under-valued, and disillusioned. If your efforts are not noticed, or worse minimized, why continue to investing your best energy?

Conversely, isolated from other team members, it is easy to assume that they are not putting in the same effort as you are. This can leave you feeling that you are being taken advantage of and carrying the weight of the team. Resentments can grow and trust within the team can be undermined.

Incidental check-ins

Brief encounters with team members or a partner in a shared project offers a great opportunity to ask about progress, provide some ad hoc problem-solving, or to offer encouragement. Asking about a project or task comes across as casual because the meeting is, by its very nature, unplanned. It feels like it is based on a genuine interest and desire to be helpful, rather than being controlling or checking up. The casual, happenstance nature of the interaction can ease suspicions about intentions and increase the probability of an assumption of goodwill.

Belonging

The most significant and problematic issue that emerges with remote working is the potential for becoming disconnected and disengaged with the culture of the organization. A basic human need is to "belong." There is safety in numbers and being part of a "tribe" increases the probability of survival. Belonging is so important that the ultimate punishment in many ancient cultures was to banish a person from the village. Death would soon follow expulsion from community membership.

We crave acceptance by the "tribe" and we will work hard to maintain this acceptance. Think peer pressure! You didn't outgrow it when you graduated from middle school. When you join an organization, you have a natural drive to fit in, to become a part of it, and to identify with it. Corporate cultures grow up in an organization because there is a need for the comfort of a structure and a common understanding of the mission, objectives, and values of the enterprise.

These elements of a corporate culture guide its members. It identifyies which behaviors will support and strengthen their membership with the group and what might get them banished. The corporate culture identifies the boundaries, us vs. them. A strong corporate culture can put systems in place that encourage performance, productivity, and engagement. Employees are motivated to do their best work because they are part of something that is bigger than themselves.

Culture is communicated through contact and experience. Members gently, and then not so gently, nudge each other to conform to the unspoken rules based on the core values of the organization. Symbols,

rituals, language, and stories all serve to create a sense of being a part of the whole and building strong brand loyalty. Members proudly wear shirts with the company logo to their children's soccer games.

The mechanisms for initiating new members and maintaining the connection of existing employees to the corporate culture all depend on frequent contact with the symbols, participating in the rituals, first-hand observations of values in action, celebrating organizational successes, collaborating with others to create group success, and sharing a common history through stories. All these mechanisms are hampered when contact is infrequent or strained.

When employees work remotely, there is a serious risk that they will not be fully initiated into the corporate culture or the bonds will become tenuous over time.

For the individual, the consequences of a weak connection with the corporate culture is a growing disengagement with the organization and, in time, a search for "tribe" membership in another organization. For the organization, a disengaged workforce is disastrous. Disengaged workers are less likely to cooperate with one another, they are more likely to engage in corporate sabotage, absenteeism soars, productivity slows, and turnover increases.

> Working from home makes it much harder to delineate work time from personal time. I encourage all of our employees to have a disciplined schedule for when you will work, and when you will not, and to stick to that schedule.
>
> *Dan Springer, CEO of DocuSign*

Chapter Four
The 10 Best Practices for Managing Remote Workers

◇◇◇◇◇◇◇◇◇◇◇◇◇◇◇◇◇◇◇◇◇◇◇◇◇◇◇◇◇◇◇◇◇◇◇

The good news

With some atten-tion to a few simple practices, you and your team can enjoy the upside of remote working and mini-mize or even elim-inate the potential downsides. Geese fly in a v-formation because when their  wings flap, it helps the goose behind and together, the entire flock is stron-ger for this shared effort. Some simple strategies, well executed, can pro-duce the same effect for your team. It isn't technical, or even difficult. It's simply a matter of awareness and then putting some systems in place.

When you implement the following strategies, you will see an immediate difference in productivity, cooperation, and engagement.

1. Touch-base contacts.

A touch-base contact is simply a deliberate interaction with your direct report for the express intent of sharing and enjoying some small talk. These can be brief 5-10 minute conversations and can be focused on checking in with each other on any important personal events or just chatting about local sports teams.

The content is light and can begin with a simple question like, "Hey, how are things going?" A touch-base contact can be an independent interaction, or it can precede a more formal conversation about a project or task. Regular weekly or bi-weekly check-ins can help each participant to see the other as a whole person and not simply as a supervisor or a direct report.

If you have not been initiating these kinds of informal chats, it might feel awkward when you first get started. That's alright, you are just being human. A good way to begin is to explain to your team what you are doing and why. You can share with them the importance of treating each other with some warmth as opposed to just seeing each other as necessary instruments for getting things done.

Trust is an essential component of a healthy, collaborative relationship and we are wired to mistrust strangers. It isn't that we have to be BFF's or get deeply into each other's private business, but it does help our working relationship to be in touch with the things and events that are most important to each other. Sharing what we are comfortable with sharing allows others to support us when we need and want it, and it offers us the opportunity to demonstrate to others that they matter to us.

A good rule-of-thumb for touch base contacts would be at least one five-minute chat every two weeks with each member of your team. Using these chats as an opener to more serious, scheduled conversations about business tasks is a nice, easy way of integrating them into your schedule. Obviously, if you can manage touch-base chats more frequently, it would be better than the suggested rule-of-thumb. But, keep in mind, as with anything, there can be too much of a good thing! Time spent touching base should not consume so much of your schedule that it interferes with your ability to get essential tasks done. Nor should it result in your needing to do more work in the evening when you should be recharging your energy for the next day.

2. Be intentional with each contact.

As important as informal contacts are, the lion's share of our communications with team members are scheduled meetings. The key to getting the most out of these exchanges is to be intentional about them.

What is the purpose of the meeting and what materials or resources will be needed to make decisions? Having an agenda and identifying what outcomes are expected from the contact are essential. This applies to group video-conference meetings as well as to meetings with individuals.

Being clear about the purpose and expected outcomes for each meeting will naturally result in fewer meetings. This little exercise will lead to your questioning the value of your own and your direct reports participation in each meeting. Don't be afraid to decline a meeting, or delegate participation in a meeting to someone else, so that both everyone's time is best used.

Pulse-check conversations

An interesting cross between intentional and touch-base contacts is a pulse-check conversation which is based on the weekly responses to a brief survey. The 3-4 question survey can be tailored to your needs but typically include questions like:

- What has gone well this week?
- What has been a challenge this week?
- What are you most proud of this week?
- Is there anything I did this week that made your job easier/harder?
- What should I be aware of that I am not?
- Do you have any advice or requests on actions I should take?
- What are your priority tasks/projects for the upcoming week/period?
- On a scale from 0-10, how satisfied are you with your job? (0 being not all, and 10 being completely satisfied.)

These are just a sample of the kind of questions you might ask. You can tailor your questions to your own group's needs but don't be tempted to use all of the above questions or to ask too many of your own. Less is better, so be careful to ask only 4-5 questions. It shouldn't take more than a few minutes to respond. Each week or every other week, on a consistent day of the week, you can send out this pulse survey, review the answers, then meet with your direct report to discuss their answers and make plans.

A tool like this will keep you in touch with how your team is feeling, what their issues or challenges are, and what people are getting done. It also gives you an opportunity to recognize the work people are doing.

Reporting sessions

Regularly scheduled reporting sessions are another useful tool for keeping track of what people are doing, where they are encountering success, and where they need your help in problem-solving. The reporting session should occur at least once a month and include coaching and feedback. A summary of activities, completed tasks, ongoing projects, plans for the future, and personal development goals should form the skeleton of the agenda. Other items can be added as needed.

The pulse-check in conversation could be integrated into this agenda and the meeting could begin with a touch-base, informal chat. Clearly these tools are not mutually exclusive, and each can make the other more powerful.

3. Use your technology.

In the last few years, technology designed for communication and collaboration has advanced dramatically. The telephone and email are great tools but for effective supervision of remote workers they are not enough. You need file sharing capability, instant messaging, electronic whiteboards, discussion boards, and video-conferencing. It is well worth your time to master these tools and then support your team using them.

Although not as complete as a face-to-face meeting, video-conferencing will give you a little more information about the emotional state or physical well-being of the other party. It doesn't work, however, if the camera is turned off. You can model appropriate use of this tool by always having your own camera on and requesting the other party, or other parties in the case of a group meeting, **to turn their cameras on**.

When using video-conferencing, pay attention to what is in your background. A pile of laundry or toys strewn all around will not leave a positive impression. Take a look to see what others will see. What do you have hanging on the walls? What furniture is in the background? An ironing board or a bed is not presenting a professional image. Some people resort to using a virtual background but there is a difference of opinion on how appropriate this is. Seeing you in front of a beach scene or in an office that is clearly not your own can be distracting, particularly if part of your hand or, worse, your head disappears every time you move. Sometimes just shifting the angle of your camera can create a positive change to what is seen in the background.

You will want to pay attention to lighting. Too much background lighting can wash your image out and others will see only a dark, ghost-like image. This can be annoying and certainly distracting. You can make a big difference by placing a lamp so that it sits just above your camera and making sure that windows have appropriate curtains to control light.

Something else to consider is the location and quality of your camera. Some laptops have the camera located at the bottom of the screen. The result is that your audience is looking up at your nostrils, which is not a great look! Also make sure that your entire head is on screen. Seeing someone from the eyes up or the nose down is irritating.

Even if your camera is at the top of your screen, cameras installed in even the most expensive laptops do not match the quality of even the cheapest webcams. Since webcams are plug and play, requiring only a USB slot, it might be worth investing in a personal webcam. This will allow you more versatility in where you place your camera, in ensuring that you have proper light, and that your entire face appears on camera.

4. Celebrate.

Birthdays, holidays, and work anniversaries are common events that teams usually celebrate. The nature of these celebrations can be varied but the power of "breaking bread" with one another can not be understated. When we eat in the presence of others, oxytocin is released in our bodies. This hormone is sometimes called the "love" hormone because it helps us to feel connected to others. It can literally build trust.

The release of oxytocin alone should be enough reason to ensure that there are opportunities to celebrate events, but added to this are the shared memories. They contribute to the stories of the group and create a stronger sense of group identity and membership.

Celebrating milestones, holidays, or birthdays might be more difficult when working with remote workers, but it is not impossible. Sending out swag bags with treats that all will share while on screen can be effective but don't be afraid to schedule a face-to-face event. You might meet at the office and have the event catered or agree to meet at a local restaurant. Whatever the choice, be sure to look for ways to celebrate, as a team, at least 3-4 times per year.

5. Schedule some face-to-face time.

Related to celebrations is the need to meet face-to-face, on occasion. Full-time remote work does not mean that the worker *never* sets foot on the corporate campus.

Ideally, there should be a block of time at least once a month in which all members of the team are required to meet in the office. For those folks whose primary workspace is at home, there might not be a desk or computer designated exclusively for their use at the office. This is not a stumbling block because most organizations will anticipate this problem and provide shared spaces, often referred to as "hoteling."

Remote workers should expect to come into the office for several activities such as: regular team meetings and for technical or leadership training. Also, occasionally to meet with colleagues with whom they are sharing a project, or as requested by you or other leaders in the organization.

While any one of these meetings might take only a small part of the day, staying for the entire day is a good idea. Being in the office for an extended period will give the worker an opportunity to catch lunch or coffee break with colleagues, to maximize productivity by avoiding the disruption of travel in the middle of the day, and it will facilitate some chance meetings with other employees. Just being in the building for an extended period of time is a subconscious reminder of the "tribe" to which they belong.

6. Communicate using multiple channels.

It has been known for a long time that different people prefer to get their information via different senses. Some people are visual and prefer to read, others prefer listening and need auditory input, and a third group gathers information kinesthetically - through sensory touch.

Added to people's different preferences for receiving information, we now also have a plethora of channels for sending out information. Some people never miss an email, others prefer to batch them and read them all at once. Some love social media, others avoid it completely. Instant messaging is a favorite for some and annoying for others. Information posted on the organizations intranet is a reliable vehicle for getting information to most employees, but not for all. An old school newsletter is just the ticket for some and while others prefer reading a blog.

To make things even more complicated, when a person is feeling a stressed, their ability to take in information is hampered. The result is that they might need to be exposed to the same message several times before it registers with them. This means that if you sent an email or posted a message on the group discussion board you cannot count on the fact that that your direct reports have seen the information, much less understood it.

When working with remote workers, you have many channels available to you and the more channels you use, the higher the probability that your messages will be delivered.

7. Create opportunities for peer-to-peer mentoring and collaboration.

When working with your remote workers, it might be easy to slip into a mindset where you see them each in an isolated pod. This is not right. They are still a team and it will be to your advantage to encourage and support a sense of team belonging.

You can facilitate teaming by encouraging team members to reach out to one another to get answers to questions or to offer information. Some times it is easier for them to admit to a colleague that they don't know something or that you are struggling with a problem than it is to admit it to you, the supervisor.

You can also assign projects to two or more team members that will require that extensive collaboration between them to complete the project. A challenge, shared with others and successfully completed, creates a strong bond. Finally, you can encourage team members to check in on each other. You might even schedule time in their weekly routines for this kind of activity.

8. Know your people: one size does not fit all.

The saying "different strokes for different folks" is particularly important when working with remote employees. Some folks are most productive in the morning, some later in the day. Some folks love to be interrupted and others feel totally distracted by interruptions and resent the time it takes to re-focus on the task.

Some prefer to communicate by telephone and others never answer voice-messages because they hate using the phone. When you assign a task, some folks will want specific instructions and a detailed description of what success looks like. Others simply want to know what the end result should look like and be allowed to plan their own path.

The more you know the different needs and preferences of your direct reports, the more you can tailor your interactions to create the optimum conditions for them to do their best work. Some of these needs and preferences can be identified by how they respond to you but, when working with remote workers, simple observations are hard to come by.

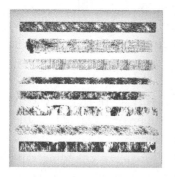 There are two simple strategies you can use to understand the needs, preferences, and strengths of your direct reports. The first is to create a simple set of questions and ask them. For example: Do you prefer an instant message or a telephone call? Is there a time of day when it would be less disruptive for me to call or would you prefer for me to call whenever I think of something I need to talk to you about? Asking questions like this demonstrates respect for individual differences and increases the probability that the communication will be well received.

Another great way to understand the needs, preferences, and strengths of your direct reports is to use standardized personality and strengths assessments. Each of these tools provides you different information and when you combine the information from two or more, you begin to see the individuality of each team member. A bonus benefit is that you can bring the team together to share their different profiles. This can lead to more patience with differences between members, allow folks to adjust their communication and behavior to maximize effectiveness, and to leverage the different strengths of team members to accomplish better outcomes.

9. Ensure that there are opportunities for growth.

Earlier it was said, "Out-of-sight, out-of-mind." In terms of professional development this also holds true, and it is dangerous. At one time there was an unwritten contract between employees and employers that, if the employee gave loyalty and hard work, the employer would ensure continued employment.

The years of downsizing and right-sizing has destroyed his contract. Most employees now understand that for their own survival, they need to be in the business of "me." What this means is that they will stay with an employer only for as long as their employer is meeting their needs.

One very important need is to remain marketable in the competitive employment arena. Things are changing rapidly and staying competitive means that skills need to be upgraded continuously. Employees want to feel that they are growing in either responsibility or in marketable skills. Any employer who ignores this need will find that their best players are moving on to other employers or positions and they are then left operating with their bench warmers. Not a good situation.

The fix for this is remarkably easy. It begins with having a conversation with your direct report about their goals and interests, creating a plan for achieving these goals or accessing their interests more frequently, and then executing the plan. This is so easy that the conversation isn't necessarily required. Just simply negotiating a plan with your direct report for one or two professional development experiences each year will get you where you want to go.

The best part of this is that, being a remote worker doesn't change anything. It is just as easy to do with a remote worker as with a worker you frequently see in the office. Projects that stretch skills, conferences, classes, or even working through a book together can all serve as professional development. The possibilities are as varied as the people involved. It's just a matter of taking a small amount of time to think about this and then putting it down on paper. A good time to do it is when you are doing your annual review. Every team member should have two things attached to their review: a list of their accomplishments for the year and a professional development plan with at least two items on it.

10. Recognize effort and accomplishments.

No one outgrows the need for recognition. Certainly, we do learn to set our own standards and congratulate ourselves when we achieve those standards – that's called "internal rewards." But, if you say that internal reward - just knowing that you did well - is all you need, you are seriously misunderstanding your own physiology.

Everyone craves an occasional atta-boy or atta-girl. When our effort or accomplishment is recognized, the brain releases a hit of dopamine. John Mendina refers to this as a "dopamine lollipop," because we love it in the same way we loved the lollipop the doctor gave us after a shot. Dopamine is often called the "more-ish" hormone because we always want more of it.

As a supervisor, you want to understand this connection. We will want to repeat whatever behavior resulted in a dopamine surge because we want more of the dopamine. An occasional comment about a behavior you like and want to see more of can go a long way towards motivating someone to give you more of it! Ken Blanchard advises managers that if they want consistent, top performance from their direct reports, they need to catch them doing the right thing and praise it.

Reward both effort and outcomes.

You might have noticed that I have suggested throughout that it is specific behaviors that merit the recognition, not just achievements. We cannot always control whether our effort, even when executed perfectly, will yield the desired outcomes. A salesperson, for example, can do all the right things and still not close the sale because a competitor swooped in and undercut the price. Since folks cannot always control the outcome, it is important to acknowledge and reward effort and improvement.

This appears to be pretty straightforward but even in the office environment, a supervisor can become busy and not notice effort, improvement, or accomplishments that are worthy of recognition. This becomes an even bigger issue with the remote worker. Unless you are deliberate in uncovering the effort, improvement, or accomplishment, it will be hidden. Fortunately, several of the tools which we have already discussed can help you with this.

First, if you have built a professional development plan, you have some specific things to monitor as the year rolls out. It is an easy thing to ask about progress on the professional development plan and then to reward the acquisition of a new skill or certification.

Second, if you are using the pulse-check conversation tool, one of the questions you can ask is "What are you most proud of this week?" or, "What did you accomplish this week?" These questions point directly to things that you can then recognize, formally or informally. Even a question like, "What challenges did you face in your work this week?" can point to some creative problem-solving or identify earnest effort on a task or project.

Third, as discussed earlier, you can encourage a direct report to peer-mentor another member of the team or you might tell a member of your team to reach out to a specific direct report for answers to questions. When you do this, you are announcing to the direct report, and to everyone else on the team, that you respect and value their work. Not only are you taking a task off your own plate by delegating this support and guidance to someone else, you are building their skills AND providing a sincere acknowledgement of their skill level. This isn't just a double-win, it's a triple-win.

Adjust your recognition

When it comes to recognition, it is important to know your people. What one person will find rewarding, another might find insulting or punishing. A public awards ceremony might mean the world to one person but feel extremely uncomfortable for another.

This brings to mind my own story. For me, the best reward for a job well done was to have the opportunity to share my results in a presentation to others. I loved speaking at conferences or internal training events. So, when I first became a supervisor, if one of my team suggested a creative idea for a problem, I immediately set about shaping the idea in such a way that it would make a meaningful learning opportunity that they could present at a conference or an internal training event. It was only a matter of a few months before I noticed that creative ideas from my team had dried up. When I questioned my team, they quickly explained that they didn't want to share their ideas because

I would make them speak about them to an audience.

This was a very important lesson. What you enjoy as a reward and recognition will not automatically be received as such by others! Once again, "different strokes for different folks." When supervising remote workers, you do not have the luxury of observing your direct reports body language following your attempt to recognize effort or accomplishment. If you are to avoid the mistake I made, you will need to have a conversation with each of your direct reports. What for them is a meaningful reward or acknowledgement of their work? Their answers might surprise you and many of those answers will be relatively inexpensive and easy to provide.

Chapter Five
Facilitating A Hybrid Meeting

Meetings are hard enough!

Facilitating an effective in-person meeting takes skill and practice. We have all experienced too many poorly planned and poorly managed meetings. Unfortunately, compared to a traditional in-person meeting, the risk of a hybrid meeting going off the rails and becoming unproductive, or even counter-productive is exponential.

What is a hybrid meeting?

A hybrid meeting is simply a meeting in which there is a combination of in-person attendees and remote workers attending via video-conferencing. With remote work becoming more common, the need for hybrid meetings will grow.

Compared to traditional, in-person meetings, hybrid meetings have some added issues and challenges. Without planning for some necessary accommodations for the remote worker, poor outcomes are highly probable. Not all meetings will be hybrid meetings and, when possible, you might even encourage people to come in to the office for an in-person meeting. This will not always be practical, however. When a hybrid meeting is necessary, if this new context for meetings is properly understood, they can be a great tool for collaboration.

Hybrid meeting challenges

A successful hybrid meeting takes some adjustments from both those attending the meeting in person and the remote worker. In the early days, teams were not always aware of the unique challenges a hybrid meeting would present and, as a result, some serious problems were encountered. That doesn't need to be the case. A little advance planning can make hybrid meetings as productive as a traditional, in-person meeting.

Screen fatigue

Attending a virtual meeting is hard on the eyes. The muscles around our eyes are the weakest muscles in our body and staring at a screen for long periods of time is a challenge. When you are writing or entering data, you have more control over your screen time. You can stop to look something up, take a short break by looking out into the room, or even closing your eyes for a few seconds. When you are in a meeting, however, looking away from the screen might be interpreted as not being fully present and others might question your commitment to the work.

No video-link:

A meeting is put on your calendar but because people are not used to hybrid meetings, no one thought to add the video link for the meeting. You are expected to attend the meeting, you have some input that others are going to need, you really need to hear what the others are discussing but you are blocked. Without that video link, quality decision-making is limited for both you and your team.

Feeling like a second-rate participant

Treats brought into a meeting or the simple side-chatter that occurs during a meeting can contribute to the feeling that you are not really part of the group. Added to that, in the early days, the remote workers head might be featured on a large screen, like the head of some extra-terrestrial being, over-seeing the meeting but not really part of it.

It is not unusual for resource material to be handed out during a meeting. Unless someone thought to send these materials to you in advance, you do not have access to this content. It is almost impossible to follow a discussion and to provide relevant, insightful commentary when you literally are not seeing what everyone else is seeing.

You feel forgotten

The team is having a great discussion and you have something you would like to add but you can't break in. Without the usual non-verbals that signal when another is finished talking and it is safe to interject, you risk talking over someone. Worse, you hear a pause in the conversation but because others can't easily see that you are about to talk, someone else has seizes the opportunity before you can get

Dr. M. Paula Daoust

your words out. No one thinks to stop, turn to you, and ask, "What is your perspective on this?" The result is that you are an observer, not a participant. This means that the team is not taking advantage of your knowledge and expertise.

Hampered participation

Team meetings often include "whiteboard" activities. During planning, sharing ideas, and brainstorming activities a facilitator usually keeps track of content by recording it on a flip chart or white board. Some activities might involve post-it notes attached to the wall to facilitate categorizing and re-organizing ideas.

Without some advanced planning, the remote worker's only recourse is to watch these activities and accept the fact that they cannot make any real-time contribution. They could certainly provide their perspective after the fact when they review the final meeting notes. At this point, however, it might be too late. Your contribution might be interpreted as criticism and "not being a team-player" for suggesting anything contrary to the work developed by the team.

Strategies for Successful Hybrid Meetings

All the challenges discussed in the previous section do not have to be a reality. With some forethought, many can easily be addressed. In addition, better use of existing technology, and learning to use new technology as it is developed, can eliminate or at least minimize these potential problems. Here are seven strategies to consider.

1. Reassess priorities

When an issue arises, it is too easy to call a meeting. When these urgent, ad hoc meetings are added to an already congested schedule of recurring team, project, and inter-departmental meetings, an entire day or week can be lost to "talking" with little "doing." Many of these meetings are focused on sharing information that could just as easily be handled via email. In addition, the wrong people are invited or too many people are invited. The result is that many attendees add little value to the content of the meeting. They either don't contribute, their contribution is not directly relevant to the issue, one or two people dominate the conversation or, out of boredom, people multi-task and miss essential content.

An early step in running a more effective hybrid meeting is to determine whether a meeting is even necessary. Information can be shared via email, internal snail-mail, or if your organization has access to Microsoft Teams, it can be posted in a topic channel where it is easily accessed when needed.

If you determine that a meeting is indeed necessary, the next step is to carefully consider who to invite. The need for stakeholders to be present for quality decision-making is essential but be careful not to go overboard in your effort to ensure that the right stakeholders are invited.

Where meetings are concerned, more is not better. This is applies even more in the hybrid environment. For an in-person meeting, the rule of thumb for an effective meeting is 6 – 8 participants with a maximum of 12. This guide is just as appropriate for a hybrid meeting.

Something else to consider is that, given that there is only so much screen real estate, too many participants will make each person's video smaller and smaller. At some point, if there are too many participants some will get moved to a second and third screen. When this happens, you are losing access to almost all non-verbal communication, and you might just as well return to an asynchronous problem-solving strategy.

Instead of crowding your screen with too many participants, identify who are essential to decision-making at this point in a task or project. As a task or project progresses, don't be afraid to change who qualifies as essential. It is always possible to move someone from the invited list to  the optional list. This leaves the decision to either attend or to skip a meeting in the hands of the potential attendees. Being on the optional list gives folks permission to opt out and many will be grateful for this option.

2. Start "out-there."

When you enter a meeting room, it is natural to take note of who is present and greet them with small-talk, or at least a nod. The virtual participant doesn't have the same opportunity.

An easy thing you can do, which will help everyone feel more comfortable and included, is to begin by acknowledging your remote participants.

A simple greeting, an introduction to the in-person participants if necessary, and some simple small talk can warm up the meeting immediately. Depending on the meeting and who your remote workers are, it might be appropriate to give them the floor to make their own quick introduction. You can follow this up by acknowledging those who are present in-person or asking each in-person participant to introduce themselves.

The key is to start with your virtual participants because they enter the meeting feeling like an outsider. The sooner you can create an inclusive environment, the more productive your meeting will be.

3. *Set the table.*

An experienced host or hostess knows that a successful dinner party is not just about the food. Creating the menu, preparing the food, and planning the presentation of the food are just as important as the meal itself.

Preparation is just as important for an effective meeting. The pre-work can make all the difference between wasted time and getting to good results. Some things to consider in your pre-planning are:

- Determine your purpose and the intended outcomes for the meeting and share this information with attendees. This will help to people determine whether this is a "must-attend" meeting or whether their time would be better spent on other tasks.

- Create an agenda with some thought to the time needed for each item. Doing so will help you to focus yourself and your attendees on critical issues and avoid getting side-tracked.

- Send materials in advance. This will make it easier for both in-person and virtual attendees to have the right resources and to be looking at the same content at the same time.

- Include a video-link for **all** attendees. In the new business normal, almost all meetings should include a video link and this should be available to all participants.

- Choose the room for your meeting carefully. To determine the appropriate room size, you will need to estimate how many participants will be in-person. In the old world, this wasn't an issue. If you invited 15 or 30 people to a meeting, you booked a room that fit. Now, in this new environment, you might not need the same size of room. In addition, you will need to make sure that the internet capability of a meeting room is enough for the number of remote participants you are expecting and what equipment is available in each meeting room.

- Plan how you will recap decisions and communicate the next steps to all participants. Know who is responsible for meeting minutes, who will send them out, and how members will comment on the minutes.

4. Manage the time.

- Time is money. Isn't that way they say? It's even more than that - it's about respect as well. Start your meetings on time. It rewards those who are prompt, but it has even more significance for the virtual attendee. It is a distinctly lonely feeling to log in to a meeting and find you are the only one present.

- Be faithful to the agenda. If an item was important enough to put on the agenda, it's important enough to be disciplined about other items so the time allotted to it is protected.

- Screen fatigue is a real thing. To avoid exhausting your virtual attendees, limit the length of your meeting to 50 minutes. If this is not possible, allow a 10-minute break every hour. This will give your participants eyes a rest and facilitate better participation in the meeting.

5. One person, one device: BYOD!

Bring your own device, a laptop or a tablet, to the meeting. It may seem counter-intuitive, but all participants should use the video link and log into the meeting. This will give everyone access to some useful tools and will put all participants on the same playing field. If everyone is logged into the meeting, the in-person participants can talk to each other as normal, but they will also have access to instant-messaging through the chat box. They can use this to send a message to the entire group or to a subset of the group and it will not matter whether the recipient is physically present or participating virtually.

Since it can sometimes be difficult for a virtual participant to interject a comment, question, or information, they can use the chat box. Someone in the room can then draw the team's attention to the chat post. In addition, if your software includes a virtual whiteboard, everyone can participate equally in group brainstorms or other activities that make use of a whiteboard. Finally, files or links can be posted in the chat box for immediate use by all participants.

6. Maximize participation.

As a facilitator of a meeting, you have three goals: maximize the use of the talent present; achieve quality outcomes; and, ensure that participants are committed to the decisions of the group. The best vehicle for all three of these goals is participation. As the facilitator, it's up to you to notice if you are not hearing your remote participants.

Don't be afraid to direct a specific question to your virtual attendee, it might be just the opportunity they have been looking for to add their perspective or to contribute some information. If nothing else, it will signal to them and the rest of the team that their input is valued.

Ensuring full participation by your virtual attendees will, at times, require some creativity and a willingness to experiment with technology. If you are going to do a brainstorming session or an activity that requires writing on a flip chart or whiteboard, you might want to assign someone to serve as an intermediary. Your virtual attendees can send their contributions to this person who can then stand in for them during the meeting.

There are many ways in which you can adapt how you get things done. But if you don't take some time to think about how to do it, you will be left with team members watching instead of participating. When this happens, you don't have access to their knowledge and skills. Sadly, they will also see the work done as someone else's work and have weak or no commitment to the decisions made. As Ken Blanchard said, "Those who plan the battle, don't battle the plan." You cannot afford to have bystanders!

7. Learn to use the technology.

The train has level the station. We have entered a new business environment and you cannot afford to be left behind. The technology for virtual meetings is advancing and if you haven't learned to use today's tools, it will be a lot harder to learn tomorrow's tools. Sometimes you have to go slow to go fast and, in this case, it might mean you will

have to invest time away from usual responsibilities to learn to use the new tools efficiently and effectively. It will be well worth that investment.

There is an additional reason for learning to use the new tools. Your meetings will be so much more effective when you can engage all your participants, both the in-person and your remote workers. Every member of your team is a valued resource. It is wasteful not to create the kind of environment in which everyone can do their best work. It is your responsibility, as the manager, to model the proper use of technology so that every meeting attendee can contribute their best effort.

---

*One last comment about technology.

Most video-conferencing tools allow recording. Just because you can do something, doesn't mean you should. Recording a meeting might make note-taking easier in that you can go back and review the meeting to create minutes. However, keep in mind that there might be some legal ramifications. Video records are discoverable when there is a legal issue. Think carefully about the purpose of recording a meeting before doing so. If there is a clear advantage in doing so, use this feature but do not automatically record every meeting.

People are more productive working at home than people would have expected. Some people thought that everything was just going to fall apart, and it hasn't. And a lot of people are actually saying that they're more productive now.

Mark Zuckerberg

Now that companies have built the framework – and experienced the cost and time savings associated with it – there's no real reason to turn back.

Mark Lobosco,
VP of Talent Solutions at LinkedIn

Chapter Six
The Secret Sauce

<>◇◇<>

Nothing new

As you worked through the list of 10 best practices, you might have noticed something. They are not unique to the world of remote work. They are, in fact, very good practices for any leader in any context. My hope is that they were already a part of your regular interaction with your direct

Dr. M. Paula Daoust

reports in the traditional face-to-face context.

It's all about leadership

The secret is out, the 10 best practices for supervising a remote worker are just examples of good leadership. The secret sauce is not so special. Good leadership is required regardless of the context - face-to-face or remote supervision.

The challenge is that these practices, while important in the traditional working environment, are essential in the remote working environment. A supervisor can get away with sloppy leadership in the traditional office, but with employees working remotely that same sloppiness will result in serious consequences for worker engagement, productivity, quality, and turn-over.

On the flip side, small changes can have big results. You don't have to immediately up your game on all ten practices. If you make an earnest effort on one or two, you will see some immediate positive results. In fact, I would urge you not to try to implement all ten changes at once. You will overwhelm yourself, become discouraged, confuse your team, and do more damage than good. Paul Lencioni argues that if "everything is important, then nothing is important."

With this thought, pick one or two things you feel comfortable with adding to your routine and get started. When you have implemented these small changes and are beginning to reap the rewards, you will be motivated to add another and then another.

Let's get started! Your work will get easier and your team will be more successful. That's a good deal! As you progress, be sure to share your strategies and results with your colleagues. You need a little recognition too and your colleagues will appreciate the help.

10 Best Practices for Managing Remote Workers

1. Frequent touch-base contacts.

2. Be intentional with each contact.

3. Use your technology.

4. Hold celebrations.

5. Schedule some face-to-face time.

6. Communicate using multiple channels.

7. Create opportunities for peer-to-peer mentoring and collaboration.

8. Know your people: One size does not fit all.

9. Ensure there are opportunities for growth.

10. Recognize effort and achievement.

7 Strategies for Successful Hybrid Meetings.

1. Reassess priorities.

2. Start "Out-there."

3. Set the table.

4. Managed the time.

5. One person - one device: BYOD!

6. Maximize participation.

7. Learn to use new technology.

References

<><><><><><><><><><><><><><><><><><><><><><><><>

Blanchard, Ken (2018) *Leading at a Higher Level: Blanchard on Leadership and Creating High Performing Teams.* 3rd Ed. FT Press.

Blanchard, Ken, and Johnson, Spencer (2015). *The New One Minute Manager.* TP Publisher

Mautz, Scott, (2018). "A 2-year Stanford Study Shows the Astonishing Productivity Boost of Working from Home: The jury was out on the productivity effect of working from home. It has returned with a surprising verdict." Inc. Magazine, April 2, 2018.

Medina, John (2014). Brain Rules: 12 Principles for Surviving and Thriving at Work, Home, and School. 2nd Ed. Pear Press.

Do you need a keynote speaker for an event?

Do you have a team or a group that is interested in building additional strength in the following topics listed below?

You can book Dr. Daoust for your event or workshop!

Managing the Remote Worker
Resolving Conflict at Work
Speaking in High-Pressured Situations
Using Emotional Intelligence in Sales
Making Change Happen with Less Stress

Other topics available on request.

DrPaula@behaviortransitions.com
www.behaviortransitions.com
785-633-6078

Made in United States
Orlando, FL
28 June 2023

34606449R00039